12 REASONS TO LOVE THE
LOS ANGELES DODGERS

by Marty Gitlin

12 STORY LIBRARY

www.12StoryLibrary.com

12-Story Library is an imprint of Peterson Publishing Company and Press Room Editions.

Produced for 12-Story Library by Red Line Editorial

Photographs ©: Chris Williams/Icon Sportswire/AP Images, cover, 1, 27; Bain News Service/Library of Congress, 4, 5, 29; Bettmann/Corbis, 7, 24; AP Images, 8, 12, 14, 15, 22; Mark J. Terrill/AP Images, 11; Bob Galbraith/AP Images, 17; David Durochik/AP Images, 19; Neal Preston/Corbis, 18; Rusty Kennedy/AP Images, 21, 28; Lenny Ignelzi/AP Images, 23; Danny Moloshok/AP Images, 25; Jack Dempsey/AP Images, 26

ISBN
978-1-63235-213-2 (hardcover)
978-1-63235-240-8 (paperback)
978-1-62143-265-4 (hosted ebook)

Library of Congress Control Number: 2015934318

Printed in the United States of America
Mankato, MN
October, 2015

Go beyond the book. Get free, up-to-date content on this topic at 12StoryLibrary.com.

TABLE OF CONTENTS

THE DODGERS BEGIN IN BROOKLYN

The Dodgers are one of baseball's oldest teams. They joined the National League (NL) in 1890. The team wasn't always called the Dodgers, though. And it wasn't always based in Los Angeles.

The team began in Brooklyn. That's a borough of New York City. Early on, the team had many nicknames. One nickname was the Bridegrooms. The team was also known for a time as the Superbas and the Robins.

The squad was first called the Dodgers in 1911.

The name came from a new type of transportation at the time. Trolley cars roared down the street much faster than the horse and carriage. Brooklyn residents were forced to

Members of the 1916 Brooklyn Robins

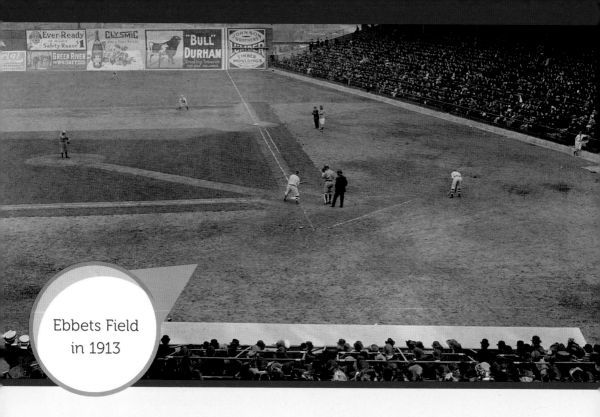

Ebbets Field
in 1913

dodge the trolleys. So the team called itself the Trolley Dodgers, or Dodgers. But still, it was not until 1932 that the nickname stuck.

The Dodgers had a colorful history in Brooklyn. By 1913, they were playing their home games at charming Ebbets Field. The cozy little ballpark made fans and players feel like they were all one big family. But people began moving away from Brooklyn. Attendance dropped. Ebbets Field became run down. Dodgers owner Walter O'Malley tried to keep the team in Brooklyn. All his attempts failed. So in 1957, he moved the Dodgers to Los Angeles.

12

NL pennants won by the Brooklyn Dodgers before moving to Los Angeles.

- The Dodgers date back to 1884.
- They played in the American Association, another major league, from 1884 to 1889.
- The NL began in 1876, while the American League (AL) started in 1901.

JACKIE ROBINSON BREAKS THE COLOR LINE

It was October 1945. The United States was segregated. Black people did not have the same rights as white people. That carried over to Major League Baseball (MLB). An unofficial "color line" kept black players out of the major leagues.

Brooklyn Dodgers general manager Branch Rickey wanted to change that. He watched Negro Leagues games. Those leagues featured the best black players. Rickey saw that black players could make his team better. So he decided to sign a young shortstop named Jackie Robinson.

It was a big decision. Many people wanted Robinson to fail. That would

7

Seasons in a row in which Jackie Robinson scored at least 99 runs to begin his MLB career.

- The Dodgers led the way in signing black players.
- Future hall of fame black catcher Roy Campanella debuted in 1948.
- Star black pitcher Don Newcombe joined the Dodgers in 1949.
- Newcombe won the NL Cy Young and MVP awards in 1956.

THINK ABOUT IT

Put yourself in Branch Rickey's position. Pretend you are looking for a black player to break the color line. What qualities would you look for in that player? Why are those qualities so important?

justify the color line. Rickey knew those people would make the transition hard for Robinson. But Rickey picked Robinson for a reason. He knew Robinson could play with the best *and* withstand the bad treatment. And he was right.

Robinson joined the Dodgers in 1947. That made him the first black player in the major leagues since the 1800s. And he was really good. Robinson batted .297 and scored 125 runs. He even led the league with 29 stolen bases. That earned him the NL Rookie of the Year Award. The Dodgers won the pennant that year. Two years later, Robinson was the NL Most Valuable Player (MVP). Later he was inducted into the Baseball Hall of Fame.

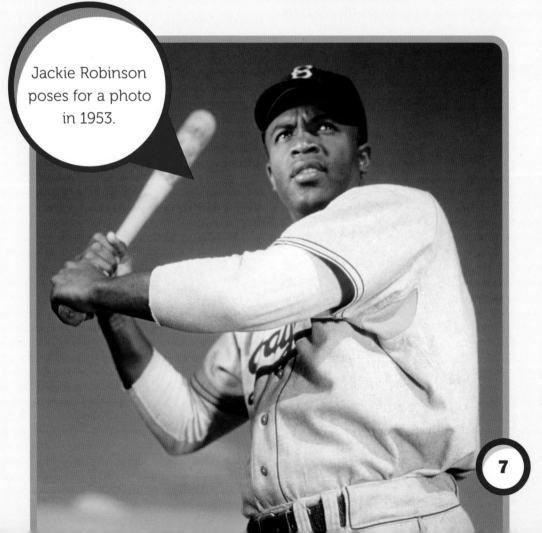

Jackie Robinson poses for a photo in 1953.

3

THE DODGERS FINALLY HIT THE TARGET

The Dodgers reached the 1955 World Series. Most baseball fans didn't have much hope for the team, though. Brooklyn was playing the crosstown New York Yankees. And the Yankees had beaten the Dodgers in the Fall Classic five times in the previous 15 years.

The Yankees won the first two games in 1955 on their home field. It seemed as though Brooklyn was doomed. But the Dodgers fought

Catcher Roy Campanella (39) lifts pitcher Johnny Podres after the Dodgers won the 1955 World Series.

9

Home runs hit by the Dodgers in the 1955 World Series.

- The win was Brooklyn's first in eight World Series appearances.
- Dodgers pitcher Johnny Podres was named World Series MVP.

back. They won the next three games at home at Ebbets Field. Sluggers Roy Campanella and Duke Snider led the way. That pair combined to smash five home runs in those games. The Dodgers were on the verge of breaking the curse against the Yankees.

Then New York won Game 6. That tied the series at 3–3. The home team had earned victories in every game to that point—and Game 7 was at Yankee Stadium. But Dodgers left-hander Johnny Podres ended that trend. He shut out the mighty Yankees 2–0. Dodgers fans waiting their entire lives to celebrate a championship finally got their wish.

THE AMAZING SNAG OF SANDY AMOROS

It was the sixth inning in Game 7 of the 1955 World Series. Brooklyn led the Yankees 2–0. But trouble was brewing. The Yankees had runners on first and second with nobody out. Yankees slugger Yogi Berra slammed a line drive down the left field line. Dodgers left fielder Sandy Amoros sprinted into the corner, extended his arm out, and snagged the ball. Amoros then whirled around and fired it back to the infield. He caught the runner off first base for a double play. The Yankees never recovered. The Dodgers went on to win their first World Series title. But they might have lost if not for Amoros.

VIN SCULLY BRINGS THE DODGERS TO FANS

Vin Scully began announcing Brooklyn Dodgers games on the radio in 1950. He called the Dodgers' first World Series win in 1955. He broadcast the first Dodgers game in Los Angeles on April 18, 1958. He called the first World Series won by the Los Angeles Dodgers in 1963.

Scully was behind the microphone when a Dodgers opponent made history in 1974. The Atlanta Braves' Hank Aaron broke baseball's all-time home run record against the Dodgers. Scully called Dodgers records, too. He announced the 1988 games in which Dodgers pitcher Orel Hershiser pitched a record 59 scoreless inning in a row.

And in 2015, Scully was still broadcasting Dodgers games on TV and the radio at the age of 87. He also announced games on national TV in the 1970s and 1980s.

Scully greeted fans on the air the same way for nearly 60 years. "It's time for Dodger baseball!" he said. "Hi, everybody, and a very good evening to you, wherever you may be."

It has always been a good evening for Dodgers fans listening to Vin Scully. Many fans tune in to Dodgers broadcasts just to hear his legendary voice.

3

Cents it cost to buy a postage stamp when Vin Scully began announcing Dodgers games in 1950.

- Scully is nicknamed "The Voice of the Dodgers."
- The 2015 season was Scully's 66th with the Dodgers.

Vin Scully at Dodger Stadium in 2007

WORKING SOLO

Most broadcasters today work in pairs. One is a play-by-play caller. This announcer shares the action that takes place in the game. The other broadcaster is an analyst. He or she explains how or why things are happening. In 2015, Vin Scully remained alone in the broadcast booth. His style gives listeners the feeling that Scully is talking directly to them.

THINK ABOUT IT

What qualities are most important for a baseball announcer? Do you value storytelling or analysis more? Use examples to explain your answer.

THE DODGERS MOVE TO THE WEST COAST

The Dodgers thrived for many years in Brooklyn. Times had changed by the 1950s. Millions of Americans had moved from the cities to the suburbs. Such was the case with many Dodgers fans. Meanwhile, more families were buying TVs. They could watch Dodgers games from home. Ebbets Field often felt empty. Fans who attended games found it to be run down and falling apart.

On the other side of the country, the West Coast was booming. California had the second-largest population of

A Dodgers fan waves a flag in a near-empty Ebbets Field on September 22, 1957.

any state. But it had no MLB team. So Dodgers owner Walter O'Malley did something about it. He took his team to Los Angeles. Another New York team went west, too. The New York Giants moved to San Francisco that year.

Many Brooklyn fans cried when the team moved in 1957. Among them was author John Thorn. He recalled the pain he felt. "I [pretended] that they were going away for a holiday but would soon be back," he said.

But the Dodgers were gone for good. And they attracted more fans in Los Angeles than they ever had in Brooklyn.

6,702

Fans who attended the last Brooklyn Dodgers game at Ebbets Field on September 24, 1957.

- The Dodgers beat the Pittsburgh Pirates 2–0 that night.
- A crowd of 78,672 watched the Dodgers' first game in Los Angeles.
- They beat the San Francisco Giants 6–5 on April 18, 1958.

THE BIGGEST CROWD EVER

The largest attendance in baseball history was for a game that didn't count in the standings. It took place on March 29, 2008, at the Los Angeles Memorial Coliseum. The exhibition game between the Dodgers and Boston Red Sox drew an incredible 115,300 fans. The previous MLB record was another Dodgers exhibition game at the Coliseum. On May 7, 1959, some 93,013 fans showed up to watch the Dodgers play the New York Yankees. That game was a tribute to Dodgers catcher Roy Campanella. He had been disabled in a car accident.

SANDY KOUFAX SHINES IN '63

The Dodgers had high hopes for Sandy Koufax. They signed the left-hander in 1954. He debuted the next season. But he struggled to reach his potential. Koufax always had a great fastball. But he rarely knew where it was going. He simply walked too many batters to be a success.

Koufax finally blossomed in 1963. And the result was one of the greatest seasons by a pitcher in baseball history. His 25 wins and 1.88 earned-run average (ERA) led the NL. So did his 306 strikeouts. After the season, he won both the Cy Young and NL MVP awards. The season ended on a high note for the Dodgers, too. They swept the New York Yankees in the World Series. The Dodgers gave up just four runs in the four games.

Sandy Koufax pitches against the New York Yankees in the 1963 World Series.

Sandy Koufax and catcher John Roseboro celebrate winning the 1963 World Series.

That year began an incredible run for Koufax. He went 97–27 from 1963 to 1966. His ERA was the best in the NL in each of those seasons. He also led the league in wins and strikeouts in 1963, 1965, and 1966. Koufax ended his career with back-to-back Cy Young Awards in 1965 and 1966.

THINK ABOUT IT

A pitcher's won-loss record shows how his team fared when he was pitching. ERA measures the average number of runs a pitcher gives up over nine innings. Which do you think is a more accurate way to analyze a pitcher? Explain why. What other stats are useful for measuring a pitcher's performance?

382

Strikeouts posted by Sandy Koufax in 1965 to set a major league record (since broken).

- Koufax first led the NL with a 2.54 ERA in 1962.
- Koufax led the NL with 27 complete games in both 1965 and 1966.
- He led the NL in strikeouts four times.
- Koufax became the first player to throw four no-hitters (and one was a perfect game).

TOMMY LASORDA BLEEDS DODGER BLUE

It was August 5, 1954. A 26-year-old named Tommy Lasorda was making his debut for the Dodgers. He proved to be a poor pitcher. He only appeared in 26 major league games before going back to the minors for several years.

Yet Lasorda would make as big an impact on the Dodgers as anyone ever has. He worked for the team as a scout for five years. He served as a minor league manager for eight seasons. He was a coach for the Dodgers from 1973 to 1976. Then he was their manager for parts of 21 years. And at the end of 2014, he was still working for the team in the front office.

Lasorda remained a Dodger 60 years after taking the mound for them in 1954. He is always proud to give his reason for that.

"I bleed Dodger blue," he has said. "And when I die, I'm going to the big Dodger in the sky."

His greatest success was as a manager. Lasorda guided the Dodgers to four NL pennants and two World Series crowns. His teams won eight division titles in his 19 full seasons in charge.

1,599
Wins as Dodgers manager for Tommy Lasorda.

- Lasorda led Team USA to an Olympic gold medal in baseball in 2000.
- He was inducted into the Baseball Hall of Fame in 1997.
- Lasorda became only the fourth manager to lead the same team for 20 years.

Tommy Lasorda argues with an umpire during a 1986 game.

ALL ABOUT ALSTON

The Dodgers had just two managers from 1954 to 1996. The second was Tommy Lasorda. He followed Walter Alston, who guided the team from 1954 to 1976. Alston led the Dodgers to their first World Series title in 1955. He then led them to championships in 1959, 1963, and 1965. The Dodgers had just four losing seasons in 23 years under Alston.

17

GARVEY AND HIS GROUP GIVE IT ALL

Great pitching? They had it. Great defense? They had it. Great hitting? They had it. The Dodgers had it all in the 1970s and early 1980s.

The Dodgers were a complete group at the plate. First baseman Steve Garvey was their biggest star. He and third baseman Ron Cey provided power. Outfielders Reggie Smith and Dusty Baker helped. Second baseman Davey Lopes brought the speed. And they all played incredible defense.

While the Dodgers were racking up the runs, their pitchers were shutting down hitters. They used veterans

Steve Garvey makes a play at first base during the 1978 World Series against the New York Yankees.

such as Burt Hooton, Charlie Hough, Tommy John, Jerry Reuss, and Don Sutton. The Dodgers had been known for their great pitching since moving to Los Angeles. Those pitchers maintained the tradition.

It is no wonder that those Dodgers teams were among the best in baseball. The Dodgers won four NL pennants during that period. They captured the World Series crown in 1981.

Ron Cey follows through on a swing.

THINK ABOUT IT

The Dodgers were routinely competitive during the 1970s and 1980s. However, they only won a single World Series. Would their run have been better if they'd had fewer winning seasons but more championships? Explain your reasoning.

14

Winning seasons for the Dodgers in 15 years from 1969 to 1983.

- The Dodgers' only losing season during that span was in 1979, when they went 79–83.
- Their best record was 102–60 in 1974.

KIRK GIBSON SAVES THE DAY

The 1988 World Series was an all-California affair. The Dodgers won the NL pennant. The Oakland Athletics won the AL title. The winner would have statewide bragging rights. And most fans expected the powerful A's to bring the championship to Northern California.

Then the A's took a 4–3 lead in Game 1. Superstar closer Dennis Eckersley took the mound for Oakland. He almost never blew a game. And he soon retired the first two Dodgers batters. Everything was falling into place.

The Dodgers appeared doomed. Even a walk to Mike Davis brought little hope. Next up, a limping Kirk Gibson made his way to the plate. Nobody expected Gibson to play. He had an injured knee and hamstring. He could barely walk. But he somehow got his

bat on the ball. It rocketed over the fence for a game-winning home run.

Gibson rounded first base, then pumped his fist twice in celebration. The fans at Dodger Stadium went wild. They knew they had seen one of the greatest moments in baseball history. The players were inspired, too. Los Angeles went on to win the series in five games.

55,983
Attendance at Dodger Stadium when the Dodgers beat the Oakland Athletics in Game 1 of the 1988 World Series.

- Los Angeles gave up just 11 runs over the five-game series.
- Dodgers pitcher Orel Hershiser was named World Series MVP.

Kirk Gibson hobbles around the bases after his home run in Game 1 of the 1988 World Series.

THE GREAT GIBSON

Kirk Gibson had enjoyed a fine career before the 1988 World Series. The outfielder joined the Dodgers that year after nine strong seasons with the Detroit Tigers. But 1988 stood out. At age 31, he batted .290 with 25 home runs. Over 17 seasons, Gibson never made the All-Star Game. Yet he was voted the NL MVP in 1988.

OREL HERSHISER SHUTS OUT EVERYONE

In 1968, Dodgers pitcher Don Drysdale set a major league record by pitching 58 straight scoreless innings. He did not allow a run in six straight starts. It was a mark some believed would never be broken. However, another pitcher did surpass it. And that pitcher happened to be a Dodger, too.

Orel Hershiser's record-breaking streak began on August 30, 1988. He pitched nine innings against the Montreal Expos. The last four innings were scoreless. Then he shut out the Atlanta Braves. Next he shut out the Cincinnati Reds. Then he shut out Atlanta again. Hershiser then blanked the Houston Astros,

Don Drysdale pitches in his fifth consecutive shutout in 1968.

San Francisco Giants, and San Diego Padres. In total, Hershiser went through 59 innings and all of September without giving up a run. All the outings were complete games. He pitched 10 innings in the final regular-season game against San Diego. The streak officially ended in the first game of the 1989 season.

Orel Hershiser delivers a pitch during the 1988 playoffs.

He was not done frustrating hitters in 1988, though. He shut out the New York Mets in the playoffs to send the Dodgers into the World Series. There he blanked the Oakland Athletics in Game 2. He then beat the Athletics in Game 5 to clinch the title.

THINK ABOUT IT

Unlike hitters, starting pitchers only play every five games. Orel Hershiser's win against the Montreal Expos was a month before the final win against the San Diego Padres. How do you think a pitcher stays focused during his off days?

23

Games won by Orel Hershiser for the Dodgers in 1988.

- His 15 complete games in 1988 led the NL.
- Hershiser pitched for the Dodgers from 1983 to 1994, and also in 2000.

GREAT LATIN PLAYERS WEAR DODGER BLUE

Some took notice when Fernando Valenzuela took the mound late in the 1980 season. The Mexican pitcher threw 17 2/3 shutout innings to end the season. Still, nobody expected what he achieved when 1981 rolled around.

Valenzuela was unhittable to begin the year. By mid-May he had given up just two runs in seven starts.

He won all seven games. Fans flocked to ballparks around the country to watch him pitch. The success of Valenzuela began an international era in baseball. Teams battled to sign the best players outside American borders.

Latin American countries, such as the Dominican Republic, Puerto Rico, and Venezuela, had strong baseball traditions. So did Cuba. That island nation did not allow citizens to freely leave. However, some Cuban baseball players escaped to the United States to pursue their dreams.

One of them was colorful Dodgers outfielder Yasiel Puig. He debuted in early June 2013. Puig provided a spark to a team that was struggling. He batted an amazing .407 in his first 34 games as the Dodgers roared into first place.

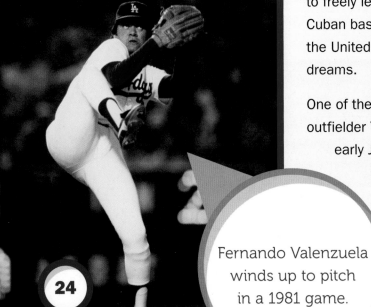

Fernando Valenzuela winds up to pitch in a 1981 game.

Every team now has many Latin American players. The Dodgers have developed one of the more successful scouting departments in Latin America. Valenzuela's success was a big reason for that emphasis.

FERNANDOMANIA!

Fernando Valenzuela was not just a sensation in Los Angeles. Attendance often doubled when he pitched on the road. After a game he pitched in Chicago, Cubs fans there began chanting, "Fernando . . . Fernando . . . Fernando!" They would not leave until Valenzuela returned to the field to wave to them.

1

Pitcher to win both the Cy Young and Rookie of the Year awards in the same year. Fernando Valenzuela did so in 1981.

- Valenzuela made six All-Star Games in his 17 seasons.
- He played 11 seasons for the Dodgers, ending in 1990.

KERSHAW BECOMES THE NEXT GREAT LEFTY

The Dodgers have featured some of baseball's best pitchers. At the top of that list is Sandy Koufax. However, another left-hander is quickly climbing the ranks.

Clayton Kershaw debuted with the Dodgers in 2008. After three solid seasons, he broke out in 2011. Kershaw had the NL's best ERA in each of the next four seasons. He compiled amazing records, such as

21–5 in 2011 and 21–3 in 2014. Plus, he led the league in strikeouts twice. Kershaw was rewarded with NL Cy Young Awards after the 2011, 2013, and 2014 seasons.

Kershaw's 2014 season was particularly impressive. His 21 wins led the NL. His 1.77 ERA was the best in the NL since 1995. In addition to the Cy Young Award, he was also named NL MVP. That made

Clayton Kershaw throws a pitch in a 2015 game.

Clayton Kershaw throws the first pitch on Opening Day in 2015.

him the first NL pitcher in 46 years to be named MVP.

Kershaw and Koufax became friends. But Koufax did not like to be compared to the modern-day ace.

"He's the first Clayton Kershaw," Koufax said. "He doesn't deserve to be compared to anybody. He is who he is and he's great."

THINK ABOUT IT

The best pitcher in each league each season wins the Cy Young Award. Meanwhile, the MVP Award usually goes to a hitter. However, sometimes a pitcher wins both. Should pitchers be allowed to win both awards? Or do you think the MVP Award should be reserved for hitters?

72
Games won by Clayton Kershaw from 2011 to 2014.

- In 2012, he was runner-up for the NL Cy Young Award.
- He also led the NL in strikeouts in 2011 and 2013.

12 KEY DATES

1890
The Brooklyn Bridegrooms win the NL pennant in their first year in the league.

1947
Jackie Robinson breaks baseball's color barrier with the Dodgers. He emerges as one of the best players in the game.

1955
The Dodgers win their first World Series by beating the New York Yankees in seven games.

1957
Owner Walter O'Malley announces he is moving the Dodgers from Brooklyn to Los Angeles.

1959
The Dodgers win their second World Series and their first in Los Angeles.

1963
The Dodgers complete a four-game sweep of the Yankees in the World Series behind superstar pitcher Sandy Koufax.

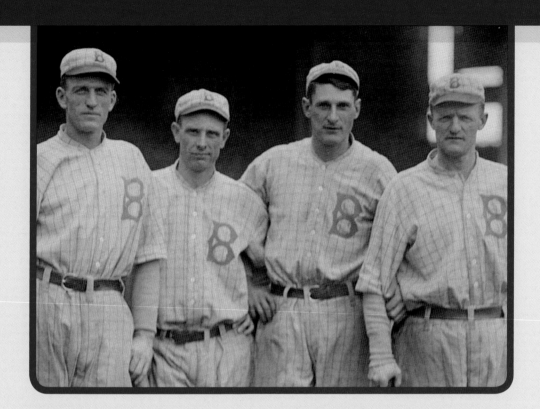

1965
Koufax leads the Dodgers to their third World Series crown in eight years since moving to Los Angeles.

1976
Tommy Lasorda begins a tremendous run as manager of the Dodgers. He manages the team for parts of 21 seasons.

1981
Phenom pitcher Fernando Valenzuela helps the Dodgers win another World Series title.

1988
Kirk Gibson hits one of the most dramatic home runs in baseball history to launch the Dodgers past the Oakland Athletics in the World Series.

2013
Cuban outfielder Yasiel Puig takes baseball by storm and helps the Dodgers reach the playoffs.

2014
Left-hander Clayton Kershaw becomes the first NL pitcher to win the MVP Award since 1968.

GLOSSARY

ace
A team's best starting pitcher.

attendance
The number of fans at a game.

borough
One of five sections of New York City.

broadcast
To show or announce an event on radio or TV.

debut
A player's first game.

exhibition
A game that does not count in the standings.

pennant
A league championship.

perfect game
A game in which a pitcher gives up no hits or walks.

scout
A person who studies players and advises a team's front office about them.

segregated
When groups of people are legally separated from one another.

shutout
A game in which the opposing team does not score a run.

trolley
A railway car or bus.

FOR MORE INFORMATION

Books

Gitlin, Marty. *Los Angeles Dodgers*. Minneapolis, MN: Abdo Publishing, 2011.

Kennedy, Mike. *Meet the Dodgers*. Chicago: Norwood House Press, 2010.

Smolka, Bo. *Jackie Robinson Breaks the Color Barrier*. Minneapolis, MN: Abdo Publishing, 2015.

Websites

Jr. Dodgers Fan Club
losangeles.dodgers.mlb.com/la/fan_forum/jrdodgers_form.jsp

Los Angeles Dodgers
losangeles.dodgers.mlb.com/index.jsp?c_id=la

MLB.com: Kids
mlb.mlb.com/mlb/kids

INDEX

About the Author

Marty Gitlin is a freelance writer based in Cleveland, Ohio. He has written nearly 100 educational books, including many about sports. Gitlin has won more than 45 awards during his 25 years as a writer, including first place for general excellence from the Associated Press. He lives with his wife and three children.

READ MORE FROM 12-STORY LIBRARY

Every 12-Story Library book is available in many formats, including Amazon Kindle and Apple iBooks. For more information, visit your device's store or 12StoryLibrary.com.